JOKES FOR KIDS

THE BEST JOKES, RIDDLES, TONGUE TWISTERS, KNOCK-KNOCK JOKES, AND ONE LINERS

WE DON'T LAUGH BECAUSE WE'RE HAPPY, WE'RE HAPPY BECAUSE WE LAUGH.

If you're like me, you love those moments that make you laugh, giggle, and chortle. My book is a collection of my all-time favorite one-liners, knock-knock jokes, and silly riddles that I told my kids as they grew up, and they still love them today.

A good sense of humor can help fix a low-time in your life, and can make the best times ever better. To the parents out there, I truly hope you enjoy this book and be sure to take a few moments to giggle and be silly with your kiddos. You'll both remember it forever.

TABLE OF CONTENTS

LOTS OF JOKES

WHAT GAS STATION DO BEES STOP AT TO USE THE BATHROOM?

the BP station

WHAT WAS WRONG WITH THE WOODEN CAR WITH WOODEN WHEELS AND WOODEN ENGINE?

It *wooden* go

WHY DO SEA-GULLS FLY OVER THE SEA?

If they flew over the bay
they would be bagels

WHAT DID THE HAMBURGER NAME HIS DAUGHTER?

Patty

WHAT HAS ONE HORN AND GIVES MILK?

A milk truck.

HOW DO YOU REPAIR A BROKEN TOMATO?

Tomato paste

WHAT WAS THE CAT IN THE HAT LOOKING FOR IN THE TOILET?

For thing number one and thing number two.

WHERE DO BULLS GET THEIR MESSAGES?

On a bull-etin board.

WHAT DID THE BLANKET SAY TO THE BED?

"Don't worry, I've got you covered"

WHAT DID THE JANITOR SAY WHEN HE JUMPED OUT OF THE CLOSET?

SUPPLIES!

WHAT DO YOU CALL A BABY MONKEY?

A chimp off the old block.

WHY WAS THE STUDENT'S REPORT CARD WET?

It was below C (sea) level

WHAT DID THE TRAFFIC LIGHT SAY TO THE CAR?

Don't look! I'm changing.

WHAT DO YOU CALL A BELT WITH A WATCH ON IT?

A waist of time

HOW DO YOU SHOOT A KILLER BEE?

With a bee bee gun

WHAT DOES A NOSEY PEPPER DO?

Gets jalepeno business!

WHY DON'T YOU SEE GIRAFFES IN ELEMENTARY SCHOOL?

because giraffes are all in High school

WHERE DID THE COMPUTER GO TO DANCE?

To a disc-o.

WHAT DO YOU CALL AN ALLIGATOR IN A VEST?

An Investi-gator

WHAT DID BACON SAY TO TOMATO?

Lettuce get together!

WHY DID THE MAN PUT HIS MONEY IN THE FREEZER?

He just wanted some cold hard cash

WHAT DO YOU GET WHEN YOU CROSS A SNOWMAN WITH A VAMPIRE?

Frostbite

WHAT WASHES UP ON VERY SMALL BEACHES?

Microwaves!

WHAT'S THE DIFFERENCE BETWEEN A FISH AND A GUITAR?

You can't tuna fish.

WHY DID THE BOY EAT HIS HOMEWORK?

His teacher said it was a piece of cake

WHY CAN'T YOU GIVE ELSA A BALLOON?

She will Let it go...let it go...

WHAT DO YOU CALL A FAKE NOODLE?

An Impasta

WHAT DO LAWYERS WEAR WHEN THEY GO TO COURT?

Law-suits

WHAT HAPPENS IF YOU EAT YEAST AND SHOE POLISH FOR BREAKFAST?

Every morning you'll rise and shine!

WHAT DID THE PENCIL SAY TO THE OTHER PENCIL?

looking sharp.

WHAT DO YOU GET WHEN YOU CROSS FISH AND AN ELEPHANT?

Swimming trunks.

WHAT IS THE MOST HARDWORKING PART OF THE EYE?

the pupil

HOW DO YOU MAKE A TISSUE DANCE?

Put a little boogey in it!

WHO EARNS A LIVING DRIVING THEIR CUSTOMERS AWAY?

A taxi driver.

WHY DID THE PICTURE GO TO JAIL?

It was framed.

WHAT HAPPENED TO THE DOG THAT SWALLOWED A FIREFLY?

It barked with de-light!

WHY DID THE COMPUTER GO TO THE DOCTOR?

It had a virus

WHY ARE FROGS SO HAPPY?

They eat whatever bugs them

WHAT KIND OF SHOES DO ALL SPIES WEAR?

Sneakers.

WHY DID THE SOCCER PLAYER BRING STRING TO THE GAME?

So he could tie the score.

WHAT DO YOU GET WHEN YOU CROSS A COW AND A DUCK?

Cheese and quackers

WHY DO FISH LIVE IN SALT WATER?

Well, pepper makes them sneeze

WHAT DID THE LEOPARD SAY AFTER EATING HIS OWNER?

Man, that hit the "spot."

WHAT DO YOU CALL A SLEEPING BULL?

A bulldozer!

WHY DID THE BANANA GO TO THE DOCTOR?

It was not peeling well

WHERE DO LIBRARY BOOKS LIKE TO SLEEP?

Under their covers

WHAT DO YOU GET FROM AN OVERLY PAMPERED COW?

Spoiled milk.

WHY DID THE BARBER WIN THE RACE?

He took a short cut

WHERE DO COWS GO ON FRIDAY NIGHT?

To the MOOOvie theater.

WHERE DO SHEEP GET THEIR WOOL CUT?

At the BAAA-bers

WHAT IS THE BEST DAY TO GO TO THE BEACH?

Sunday!

WHAT BOW CAN'T BE TIED INTO A KNOT?

Rainbows

WHAT SEASON IS IT WHEN YOU ARE ON A TRAMPOLINE?

Spring time.

WHY DID THE BELT GO TO JAIL?

It held up a pair of pants

WHY DID GOOFY PUT A CLOCK UNDER HIS DESK?

He wanted to work over-time!

WHAT DO YOU GET WHEN YOU CROSS A FRIDGE WITH A RADIO?

Cool Music.

WHAT HAS ONE HEAD, ONE FOOT AND FOUR LEGS?

A Bed

WHY WAS THE GUY LOOKING FOR FAST FOOD ON HIS FRIEND?

his friend said "dinner is on me".

DID YOU HEAR THE JOKE ABOUT THE ROOF?

Never mind, it's over your head

WHY DIDN'T THE SKELETON GO TO THE DANCE?

Because he had no-body to go with.

WHAT IS IT CALLED WHEN A CAT WINS AT A DOG SHOW?

A cat-has-trophy

WHY DID THE BABY STRAWBERRY CRY?

Because his parents were in a jam!

WHERE DO SNOWMEN KEEP THEIR MONEY?

In snow banks.

WHAT GOES THROUGH TOWNS, UP & OVER HILLS, BUT DOESN'T MOVE?

Roads

WHY WAS THERE THUNDER AND LIGHTNING IN THE LAB?

 The scientists were brainstorming

WHAT DO YOU GET WHEN YOU CROSS A CAT WITH A LEMON?

A sour puss

WHY DO BIRDS FLY SOUTH FOR THE WINTER?

It's easier than walking

WHAT DID THE FISH SAY WHEN HE SWAM INTO THE WALL?

Dam!

WHAT DO YOU CALL A FUNNY MOUNTAIN?

Hillarious

WHY COULDN'T THE PIRATE PLAY CARDS?

Because he was sitting on the deck

WHY SHOULD YOU TAKE A PENCIL TO BED?

To draw the curtains

WHAT DID ONE ELEVATOR SAY TO THE OTHER ELEVATOR?

I think I'm coming down with something

HOW DO YOU MAKE AN OCTUPUS LAUGH?

With ten-tickles

WHY CAN'T YOUR NOSE BE 12 INCHES LONG?

Because then it would be a foot!

WHAT HAS FOUR WHEELS AND FLIES?

A garbage truck

HOW MANY BOOKS CAN YOU PUT IN AN EMPTY BACKPACK?

One, because after that it is not empty anymore

WHAT KIND OF BUTTON WON'T UNBUTTON?

A bellybutton!

WHAT DID THE TRIANGLE SAY TO THE CIRCLE?

Your pointless

WHAT IS A BUBBLES LEAST FAVORITE DRINK?

Soda *pop*

WHAT STARTS WITH A P, ENDS WITH AN E, AND HAS A MILLION LETTERS IN IT?

Post Office!

WHAT DOG KEEPS THE BEST TIME?

A watch dog.

WHAT STAYS IN THE CORNER AND TRAVELS ALL OVER THE WORLD?

A stamp.

WHAT DID THE JUDGE SAY WHEN THE SKUNK WALKED IN THE COURT ROOM?

Odor in the court.

WHAT STREETS DO GHOSTS HAUNT?

Dead ends!

WHY DID THE ROBBER TAKE A BATH?

He wanted to make a clean
getaway.

WHAT DID THE PENNY SAY TO THE OTHER PENNY?

We make perfect cents.

WHY DID THE MAN WITH ONE HAND CROSS THE ROAD?

To get to the second hand shop.

WHY DID THE BOY SPRINKLE SUGAR ON HIS PILLOW BEFORE HE WENT TO SLEEP?

So he could have sweet dreams.

WHAT DO YOU CALL CHEESE THAT IS NOT YOURS?

Nacho Cheese

WHAT DID ONE PLATE SAY TO THE OTHER?

"Dinners on me"

WHAT DID THE JUDGE SAY TO THE DENTIST?

Do you swear to pull the tooth, the whole tooth and nothing but the tooth.

WHAT GOES UP WHEN THE RAIN COMES DOWN?

An umbrella.

WHAT KIND OF LIGHTS DID NOAH USE ON THE ARK?

Flood lights

DID YOU HEAR ABOUT THE RACE BETWEEN THE LETTUCE AND THE TOMATO?

The lettuce was a "head" and the tomato was trying to "ketchup"

WHY IS ENGLAND THE WETTEST COUNTRY?

The queen has reigned (rained) there for years

WHICH MONTH DO SOLDIERS HATE MOST?

March

WHY DON'T SKELETONS FIGHT EACH OTHER?

They don't have the guts.

WHY DO GOLFERS WEAR TWO PAIRS OF PANTS?

In case they get a hole in one!

WHAT DID THE STAMP SAY TO THE ENVELOPE?

Stick with me and we will go places

WHY DID TOMMY THROW THE CLOCK OUT OF THE WINDOW?

He wanted to see time fly

WHAT KIND OF EGG DOES AN EVIL CHICKEN LAY?

A deviled egg

WHAT KIND OF KEY OPENS THE DOOR ON THANKSGIVING?

A tur-key

WHY DID THE COOKIE GO TO THE HOSPITAL?

He felt crumb-y

WHY WERE THE TEACHER'S EYES CROSSED?

She couldn't control her pupils

WHAT DO YOU CALL A BEAR WITH NO SOCKS ON?

Bare-foot

WHAT CAN YOU SERVE BUT NEVER EAT?

A volleyball.

WHY IS A BASEBALL TEAM SIMILAR TO A MUFFIN?

They both depend on the batter.

HOW DO CRAZY PEOPLE GO THROUGH THE FOREST?

They take the psycho path.

WHAT DO PRISONERS USE TO CALL EACH OTHER?

Cell phones.

WHAT DID THE ALIEN SAY TO THE GARDEN?

 Take me to your weeder.

HAVE YOU HEARD THE JOKE ABOUT THE BUTTER?

I better not tell you...it might spread.

HOW DO BASEBALL PLAYERS STAY COOL?

They sit next to their fans.

WHAT DOES A SHARK LIKE TO EAT WITH PEANUT BUTTER?

Jellyfish

WHY WAS THE MATH BOOK SAD?

It had a lot of problems.

WHAT RUNS BUT DOESN'T GET ANYWHERE?

Refrigerators

WHAT IS AN ASTRONAUT'S FAVORITE KEY ON A KEYBOARD?

The Space bar

HOW DO YOU KNOW THAT CARROTS ARE GOOD FOR YOUR EYESIGHT?

Have you ever seen a rabbit wearing glasses?

WHY IS BASKETBALL SUCH A MESSY SPORT?

Because you dribble on the floor

HOW DO YOU COMMUNICATE WITH A FISH?

Drop him a line

WHERE DO SHEEP GO TO GET HAIRCUTS?

To the Baa Baa shop!

WHAT'S BLACK AND WHITE, BLACK AND WHITE, BLACK AND WHITE?

A penguin rolling down a hill!

WHAT EXAM DO YOUNG WITCHES HAVE TO PASS?

A spell-ing test

WHAT DO CATS EAT FOR BREAKFAST?

Mice Crispies

WHY CAN'T A LEOPARD HIDE?

Because he's always spotted

WHAT DO YOU GIVE A DOG WITH A FEVER?

Mustard, its the best thing for a hot dog

WHAT KIND OF KEY OPENS A BANANA?

A mon-key

WHY DID THE BOY TIPTOE PAST THE MEDICINE CABINET?

He didn't want to wake the sleeping pills

WHY DOES A HUMMINGBIRD HUM?

It doesn't know the words

WHY ARE SOME FISH AT THE BOTTOM OF THE OCEAN?

Because they dropped out of school

WHY DID THE BIRD HAVE TO GO TO THE HOSPITAL?

It needed a tweetment.

WHAT SOUND DO PORCUPINES MAKE WHEN THEY KISS?

Ouch

WHAT GOES UP AND DOWN BUT DOESN'T MOVE?

The temperature

WHAT DID THE TIE SAY TO THE HAT?

You go on ahead and I'll hang around

WHAT RUNS BUT CAN'T WALK?

The faucet

WHEN IS THE BEST TIME TO GO TO THE DENTIST?

At tooth-hurty

WHAT KIND OF BED DOES A MERMAID SLEEP IN?

A water bed

WHAT KIND OF CRACKERS DO FIREMEN LIKE IN THEIR SOUP?

Firecrackers

HOW DO BULLS PAY WHEN THEY GO SHOPPING?

They charge

WHAT'S TAKEN BEFORE YOU GET IT?

Your picture.

WHY DID THE TREE GO TO THE DENTIST?

it needed root canal

WHY WAS THE BROOM LATE?

It over swept!

WHY COULDN'T KIDS GO TO THE PIRATE MOVIE?

Because it was rated arrrrr

WHAT'S THE DIFFERENCE BETWEEN MS. AND MRS.?

A Mr.

WHY CAN'T A BICYCLE STAND UP BY ITSELF?

Because it's two-tired

WHAT DID THE NOSE SAY TO THE FINGER?

Stop picking on me.

WHAT DID THE PAINTER SAY TO THE SARCASTIC WALL?

One more crack like that and I'll plaster you

WHO CLEANS THE BOTTOM OF THE OCEAN?

A Mer-Maid

WHAT DID THE GRAPE DO WHEN IT GOT STEPPED ON?

It let out a little wine

WHAT PLANT GIVES THE BEST KISSES?

Tulips (two-lips)

WHY DID THE GIRL BRING LIPSTICK AND EYE SHADOW TO SCHOOL?

She had a make-up exam

WHY DID THE CHICKEN CROSS THE PLAYGROUND?

To get to the other slide.

WHAT DO YOU CALL A RABBIT WITH FLEAS?

Bugs Bunny

WHY DID THE GIRL BRING LIPSTICK AND EYE SHADOW TO SCHOOL?

She had a make-up exam

NAME A CITY WHERE NO ONE GOES?

Electricity

WHAT'S THE DIFFERENCE BETWEEN A CAT AND A FROG?

A Cat has nine lives but a Frog croaks every night

WHY CAN YOU NEVER TRUST ATOMS?

They make up everything

WHERE DOES BAD LIGHT GO?

To prism

WHAT DO YOU CALL A PIG THAT KNOWS KARATE?

A pork chop

WHY DO BEES HAVE STICKY HAIR?

They use honeycombs.

WHY WAS THE MAN RUNNING AROUND HIS BED?

He wanted to catch up on his sleep.

WHY IS 6 AFRAID OF 7?

Because 7 8 9 (7 ate 9)

WHY DO COWS WEAR BELLS?

Their horns don't work

HOW DO YOU MAKE A TISSUE DANCE?

Just put a little boogie in it.

WHERE DOES A TREE STORE THEIR STUFF?

In their trunk of course

RIDDLES

REAL RED REDWOOD TREES: CAN YOU SPELL THAT WITHOUT ANY "R'S"?

T-H-A-T

HOW DO YOU CALL A NO-LEGGED DOG?

It doesn't matter, he won't come anyway.

WHICH WEIGHS MORE, A TON OF FEATHERS OR A TON OF BRICKS?

Neither, they both weigh one ton.

HOW DO YOU SAY "YELLOW JELLYBEANS TASTE GREAT" BACKWARDS.

First, face the other way, then say:
"Yellow jellybeans taste great"

WHAT GETS WETTER THE MORE IT DRIES?

A towel.

IF YOU ARE RUNNING IN A RACE AND YOU PASS THE PERSON IN 2ND PLACE, WHAT PLACE ARE YOU IN?

2nd place.

WHAT BELONGS TO YOU BUT OTHER PEOPLE USE IT MORE THAN YOU?

Your name.

IF I HAVE IT, I DON'T SHARE IT. IF I SHARE IT, I DON'T HAVE IT. WHAT IS IT?

A secret.

WHAT HAS A FACE AND TWO HANDS, BUT NO ARMS OR LEGS?

A clock.

WHAT HAS TO BE BROKEN BEFORE YOU CAN USE IT?

An egg.

WHAT GOES UP AND NEVER COMES DOWN?

Your age.

WHAT CAN RUN BUT CAN'T WALK?

A drop of water.

HOW CAN A PERSON GO 8 DAYS WITHOUT SLEEP?

 Only sleep at night.

I'M FULL OF KEYS BUT I CAN'T OPEN ANY DOOR. WHAT AM I?

A piano.

WHAT GETS ANSWERED BUT NEVER ASKS A QUESTION?

A doorbell.

I'M LIGHTER THAN A FEATHER, BUT
NO ONE CAN HOLD ME FOR MORE
THAN A FEW MINUTES. WHAT AM I?

Breath.

WHAT KIND OF COAT HAS TO BE WET
TO BE PUT ON?

A coat of paint.

WHEN YOU LOOK FOR SOMETHING,
WHY IS IT ALWAYS IN THE LAST
PLACE YOU LOOK?

Because you stop looking once you find it.

I'M TALL WHEN I'M NEW AND I'M SHORT WHEN I'M OLD. WHAT AM I?

A candle.

A COWBOY RODE INTO TOWN ON FRIDAY. HE STAYED IN TOWN FOR THREE DAYS AND RODE OUT ON FRIDAY. HOW WAS THAT POSSIBLE?

His horse was named Friday.

WHAT OCCURS ONCE IN A MINUTE, TWICE IN A MOMENT, AND NEVER IN ONE THOUSAND YEARS?

The letter M.

WHAT HAS THREE FEET BUT CANNOT WALK?

A yardstick.

JIM'S MOTHER HAD FOUR CHILDREN. THE FIRST WAS NAMED JANUARY, THE NEXT WAS NAMED FEBRUARY, THE THIRD MARCH. WHAT WAS THE NAME OF THE FOURTH CHILD?

Jim

WHAT IS AT THE END OF A RAINBOW?

The letter W.

WHAT RUNS, BUT NEVER WALKS, NEVER TALKS, HAS A BED BUT NEVER SLEEPS, HAS A MOUTH BUT NEVER EATS?

A river.

WHAT CAN YOU CATCH BUT CANNOT THROW?

A cold.

WHAT LIVES IN WINTER, DIES IN THE SUMMER, AND IT GROWS UPSIDE DOWN?

An icicle.

WHAT IS FULL OF HOLES BUT CAN STILL HOLD WATER?

A sponge.

WHAT HAS A THUMB AND FOUR FINGERS BUT IS NOT ALIVE?

A glove.

THE MORE YOU TAKE, THE MORE YOU LEAVE. WHAT ARE THEY?

Footprints

WHAT HAS HANDS BUT CANNOT CLAP?

A clock.

WHAT COMES OUT AT NIGHT WITHOUT BEING CALLED, AND IS LOST DURING THE DAY WITHOUT BEING STOLEN?

Stars

WHAT INVENTION LETS YOU LOOK THROUGH A WALL?

A window.

HOW MANY MONTHS HAVE 28 DAYS?

All 12 months.

KNOCK-KNOCK JOKES

KNOCK, KNOCK.

Who's there?

BANANA.

Banana who?

KNOCK, KNOCK.

Who's there?

ORANGE.

Orange who?

ORANGE YOU GLAD I DIDN'T SAY
BANANA?!

KNOCK KNOCK.

Who's there?

COW SAYS.

Cow says who?

NO, A COW SAYS MOOOOO!

KNOCK, KNOCK

Who's there?

ORANGE

Orange who?

ORANGE YOU GOING TO ANSWER THE DOOR?

KNOCK KNOCK.

Who's there?

CANOE.

Canoe who?

CANOE COME OUT OR WHAT?

KNOCK! KNOCK!

Who's there?

NANA.

Nana who?

NANA YOUR BUSINESS WHO'S THERE.

KNOCK KNOCK.
Who's there?
CANDACE.
Candace who?
CANDACE DOOR OPEN, OR WHAT?

KNOCK! KNOCK!
Who's there?
DOZEN.
Dozen who?
DOZEN ANYONE WANT TO LET ME IN?

KNOCK KNOCK.
Who's there?
OLIVE.
Olive who?
I LOVEOU!

KNOCK, KNOCK.

Who's there?

BOO.

Boo hoo?

IT'S JUST A JOKE, WHY ARE YOU CRYING?

KNOCK KNOCK.

Who's there?

ETCH.

Etch who?

BLESS YOU!

KNOCK, KNOCK

Who's there?

I AM

I am who?

YOU DON'T KNOW WHO YOU ARE?

KNOCK KNOCK.

Who's there?

TANK.

Tank who?

YOU'RE WELCOME.

KNOCK, KNOCK

Who's there?

RADIO

Radio who?

RADIO NOT, HERE I COME!

KNOCK KNOCK.

Who's there?

YA.

Ya who?

YAHOO! I'M EXCITED TO SEE YOU!

KNOCK KNOCK.

Who's there?

SPELL.

Spell who?

ALRIGHT: W. H. O.

KNOCK KNOCK

Who's there?

WATER.

Water who?

WATER YOU DOING? JUST OPEN THE DOOR!

KNOCK KNOCK.

Who's there?

CASH.

Cash who?

NO THANKS, I'LL HAVE SOME PEANUTS.

KNOCK, KNOCK.
Who's there?
HOO.
Hoo who?
ARE YOU A OWL?

KNOCK KNOCK.
Who's there?
LETTUCE.
Lettuce who?
LETTUCE IN, IT'S COLD OUT HERE!

KNOCK KNOCK.
Who's there?
A LITTLE OLD LADY.
A little old lady who?
**ALL THIS TIME, I HAD NO IDEA YOU
COULD YODEL.**

KNOCK KNOCK.

Who's there?

SAYS.

Says who?

SAYS ME, THAT'S WHO.

KNOCK, KNOCK!

Who's there?

COOK.

Cook who?

WHO ARE YOU CALLING CUCKOO?!

KNOCK KNOCK.

Who's there?

MUSTACHE.

Mustache who?

I MUSTACHE YOU A QUESTION, BUT
I'LL SHAVE IT FOR LATER.

KNOCK, KNOCK.

Who's there?

SOMEBODY TOO SHORT TO RING THE DOORBELL!

TONGUE TWISTERS

I THOUGHT, I THOUGHT OF THINKING
OF THANKING YOU.

STUPID SUPERSTITION.

FRESHLY FRIED FRESH FLESH.

I SCREAM, YOU SCREAM, WE ALL
SCREAM FOR ICE CREAM

TOY BOAT. TOY BOAT. TOY BOAT.

HOW MUCH WOOD WOULD A
WOODCHUCK CHUCK IF A
WOODCHUCK COULD CHUCK WOOD?
HE WOULD CHUCK AS MUCH WOOD
AS A WOODCHUCK COULD
IF A WOODCHUCK COULD CHUCK
WOOD.

GREEN GLASS GLOBES GLOW
GREENLY

ROUND THE ROUGH AND RUGGED
ROCK THE RAGGED RASCAL RUDELY
RAN.

HE THREW THREE FREE THROWS.

SHE SEES CHEESE.

LESSER LEATHER NEVER WEATHERED
WETTER WEATHER BETTER.

SHE SELLS SEA SHELLS BY THE SEASHORE.

EVE EATING EAGERLY ELEGANT EASTER EGGS.

ELEVEN BENEVOLENT ELEPHANTS.

SUSIE SITS SHINING SILVER SHOES

BETTY BOUGHT A BIT OF BUTTER.
BUT THE BUTTER BETTY BOUGHT
WAS BITTER. SO BETTY BOUGHT A
BETTER BUTTER, AND IT WAS
BETTER THAN THE BUTTER BETTY
BOUGHT BEFORE.

NINE NICE NIGHT NURSES NURSING
NICELY.

PETER PIPER PICKED A PECK OF
PICKLED PEPPERS.
A PECK OF PICKLED PEPPERS PETER
PIPER PICKED.
IF PETER PIPER PICKED A PECK OF
PICKLED PEPPERS?
WHERE'S THE PECK OF PICKLED
PEPPERS PETER PIPER PICKED?

IF YOU NOTICE THIS NOTICE, YOU WILL NOTICE THAT THIS NOTICE IS NOT WORTH NOTICING.

A SKUNK SAT ON A STUMP AND THUNK THE STUMP STUNK, BUT THE STUMP THUNK THE SKUNK STUNK.

OLD OILY OLLIE OILS OLD OILY AUTOS

QUIZZICAL QUIZ, KISS ME QUICK.

WHICH WITCH IS WHICH?

BAKE BIG BATCHES OF BITTER
BROWN BREAD

HAVE YOU REVIEWED THIS BOOK?

Hi there! I really hope you enjoyed this book as much as I enjoyed putting it together for you. I would really appreciate it if you took a minute and made a review on Amazon to share your thoughts with other future customers.

As an independent author, I depend on readers like you to make honest, fair, and objective reviews. Your opinion matters!

Thank you!!

Made in the USA
San Bernardino, CA
16 March 2020